ALL ABOUT MY BROTHER

An eight-year-old sister's introduction to her brother who has autism

ALL ABOUT MY BROTHER

An eight-year-old sister's introduction to her brother who has autism

Written and Illustrated by Sarah Peralta

With Foreword by Brenda Smith Myles, Ph.D.

P.O. Box 23173
Shawnee Mission, KS 66283-0173

APC

© 2002 by Autism Asperger Publishing Co.,
Reprinted 2007
P.O. Box 23173
Shawnee Mission, Kansas 66283-0173

Publisher's Cataloging-in-Publication
(provided by Quality Books, Inc.)

Peralta, Sarah.
    All about my brother / Sarah Peralta. -- 1st ed.
    p. cm.
    SUMMARY: A young author tells about her brother who has autism.
    Audience: Ages 6-10.
    Library of Congress Control Number: 2002106067
    ISBN: 1-931282-11-0

    1. Autistic children--Juvenile literature.
2. Asperger syndrome--Juvenile literature. [1. Brothers--Juvenile literature. 2. Autism. 3. Brothers. I. Title.

RJ506.A9P47 2002   618.92'8982
                      QB133-525

Managing Editor: Kirsten McBride
Interior Design/Production: Tappan Design

Printed in the United States of America.

DEDICATION

I want to thank my Mom, who gave me the idea to write a book for kids. I also want to thank Ann Densmore for helping me put into words my feelings about my brother.

A special thank you to all my family and friends, especially Dad, Nana, Papa Jim, Angela, Evan G., Charlotte, her little brother, Ethan, and Kate. You guys are the best!

Most kids don't know anything about autism and don't understand some of the things that kids with autism do. Some kids are afraid of kids who are different from themselves. Sometimes they are even mean to someone who is different to show they are tough.

I hope that this book helps to teach kids about autism because once they understand, they won't be so afraid any more.

– Sarah Peralta

Sarah and Evan playing

Evan is seven years old. He is nonverbal and communicates through the use of pictographs and basic signs. Evan attends a special needs school and receives additional services at home after school hours. He is a lovable, affectionate little brother. He loves his sister very much.

FOREWORD

Sometimes we need to step back from our preconceived notions and look at things a bit differently. I don't do this often without prompting and, as a result, I miss out on learning. Without a doubt, children have been the instigators of helping me use a "different set of glasses" to view the world. The children who challenge us are bright, creative, and original. Sarah Peralta is one of these children. She is eight years old, but has wisdom beyond her years. Sarah's message is simple: seek to understand and enjoy people in your world.

I have read *All About My Brother* many times and each time I learn from Sarah. Individuals with autism are people first. They do some things well while being challenged by others. Like all other children, children with autism enjoy some activities and dislike others. Sarah's brother, Evan, is special, but he is special because he is a brother and son. He does have autism, but that is just a small piece of who he is.

Sarah demystifies autism by giving us insights into Evan's world. She clearly communicates that there is no such thing as an "autistic person." Each person is an individual. If we would all look at the world the way Sarah does, there would be no reason for people to shy away from what they don't understand and there would be no reason for bullying programs because acceptance is the clear message. Finally, there would no reason to stereotype people and draw conclusions about someone just because they have a label.

Sarah has given us a wonderful gift. I hope that we can live up to its expectations. If we can, the world will be a better place.

– Brenda Smith Myles, Ph.D.
Associate Professor
University of Kansas

Recent books by and with Brenda Smith Myles include *Asperger Syndrome and Adolescence: Practical Solutions for School Success, Asperger Syndrome and Sensory Issues: Practical Solutions for Making Sense of the World,* and *Asperger Syndrome and Difficult Moments: Practical Solutions for Tantrums, Rage, and Meltdowns.*

PREFACE

Parent Perspective

The idea for writing this book came from discussions I had with my daughter, Sarah, about her brother's diagnosis of autism spectrum disorder. From the start, Sarah had many questions about this perplexing disorder. For example, learning to talk is not something most people think about; it is something that just happens, and therefore is expected. So why doesn't Evan talk? Her questions were Sarah's attempt to make sense out of the confusing set of problems presented by her little brother.

As a sibling of a child with a pervasive developmental disability, Sarah has had a great deal of exposure to issues that most adults have yet to come to terms with. Initially, the most difficult questions Sarah had to ponder were, Why our family? Why my brother? Why can't Evan be like my friend's little brother? Once children move away from these initial dilemmas, they may begin to ask questions such as, How can I help him? What can I teach him?

Sarah's journey through the world of autism is just beginning, but she has made tremendous gains throughout these difficult years. As Evan's and Sarah's parent, I have focused on balancing my efforts to advocate for Evan's needs with addressing the needs of all of our family as we try to give Evan every possible opportunity to grow, learn and live his life to his fullest potential.

One of the difficulties that have come up for Sarah is trying to understand the differences between children on the spectrum and sorting out where her brother fits in. She has seen other children with the same diagnosis make strides that Evan has yet to attain. She grieves, as a parent would, trying to come to terms with the challenges her brother has. For example, she once asked if Evan ever feels sad because he has never had a play date. It is difficult to answer such a question, but it can be explained by talking about the kinds of things that make Evan happy. A play date simply isn't something that makes Evan smile.

Sarah spends a great deal of time thinking about what Evan will be like when he grows up. The answer is – we don't know. There are many more questions than answers. This is a lesson siblings of children with a developmental disability learn early on. This uncertainty brings to light that doctors, or any professionals for that matter, are not always the experts. My daughter has proclaimed herself as the one who knows Evan the best. She is the one who knows what he wants and what he is thinking. Perhaps this grandiosity is a coping strategy, but perhaps she is right. We may never know for sure.

– Dorothea Iannuzzi, MSW, LICSW
Sarah's mother

INTRODUCTION

Ever since my son's diagnosis of autism, Sarah has had a lot of questions. She is by nature an inquisitive child and her brother puzzled her. One big issue initially was, Why doesn't he want to talk to me? Why won't he play with me? Why does he ignore me? How do I know he loves me? Quite frankly, when Evan was initially diagnosed I shared many of the same concerns as Sarah. In addition, as a parent to both children, I needed to be supportive of her at a time when I had many unanswered questions myself.

As a parent I also wondered, "What did I do?" I tormented myself for quite some time trying to unlock the mystery of what had caused Evan's autism. But the energy I spent going down this dead end could have been better channeled into developing my observational skills in an effort to learn as much as possible about how Evan perceives the world around him. Such knowledge can be used to develop an educational plan that speaks to his individual information processing.

As a neurotypical child Sarah is a natural observer and imitator. Early on, if Evan started to perseverate on an object, she would try it out herself in an attempt to see what Evan sees. She made and continues to make every effort to join him where he is, rather than forcing him to conform to some standard of behavior. She teaches him every day and rarely gets discouraged at his slow progress or lack of interest.

But it is important to understand that she does get very angry with him at times, especially if he gets into her stuff. Sometimes he also embarrasses her, but she is learning how to deal with that. Recently when Sarah had a friend over, Evan decided to strip off his clothes in the kitchen and parade around wearing only his snow boots. Sarah calmly told her friend that her brother is more comfortable without his clothes rubbing on his skin. "It's a sensory thing," she explained matter-of-factly. Her friend looked puzzled but accepted the explanation without any further concern.

Sarah has made an effort to look at her brother's behaviors from a different perspective. She does not want to fix them … well, maybe sometimes. Instead, she wants to learn from them to figure out what makes her brother happy. This book illustrates the kinds of exchanges Sarah and Evan have and the areas of strength that she sees in Evan. In many ways Sarah depathologizes her brother's behavior and tries to put a positive spin on it.

– Dorothea Iannuzzi

How to Use This Book

This book is offered as a tool for parents, educators and children to use to facilitate conversation regarding children's thoughts about other children who are "differently abled," or more commonly referred to as "disabled." The book can be used in many different ways and in many different contexts, as suggested below.

10-STEP GUIDE

1. Find a quiet place free of visual and auditory distractions, and without the presence of the child with a disability.

2. Ask your child/children to draw a picture of either their family or their classroom, including the child with the disability. This drawing will help to illustrate the role the affected child has within the group. The drawing may also point out alliances and accommodations that may or may not be made to meet the needs of the child.

3. Introduce the book as a book written by a child who has a lot to say about how her life is affected by having a sibling with a disability.

4. Read through the text in its entirety and then ask for feedback.

5. Ask the child/children to draw a picture of what they liked or disliked about the book. In other words, ask them to write/draw a book review.

6. Acknowledge both the negative and the positive things the child/children come up with. It is extremely important that the negative feelings be validated and accepted. Any feelings of guilt also need acknowledgment.

7. Don't underestimate the depth of understanding that children have. Often their understanding is on a higher level than for some adults.

8. Encourage further discussion among the children as well as with the affected child if he or she is able to participate meaningfully in the discussion.

9. Facilitate a discussion of the concept of "differently abled." Discuss what abilities each of the children have and what kinds of things are difficult for them and why. (This exercise is geared for older, more verbal children.)

10. Finally, make the activity fun and never push. Gently encourage the children to process the information and engage in the discussion. If a child pulls back, respect that reaction. Try again another time.

– Dorothea and Sarah

This is my family. I have a brother named Evan, in the green shirt. He has autism. It is a complicated problem. My Mom is in the yellow shirt. My Dad is in the red shirt and I am in the orange shirt. Evan can't talk. He has never talked to me or my family using words. Instead he uses pictures and sign language. I wonder what he would say to me if he did talk to me. I have a lot to say to him, and I think he understands most of what I say.

My brother loves to play with sticks. He taps them up and down. He is very fussy about what stick he plays with. His teachers and therapists call it "stimming." All I know is that he really likes to play with sticks and tries to turn things into a stick whenever he can. Evan is always happiest when he has a stick to flick around. Playing with sticks is his favorite thing to do. I tried it once and it was fun.

I love dogs. I have a dog of my own. His name is Daniel. He is a great dog. Daniel can't talk either, but I know what he wants just by looking at his face. Evan loves to play with Daniel's tail. I think he sees it as a furry stick that moves on its own. Evan tries to catch it as it moves back and forth when Daniel wags his tail.

My Mom likes to read books and she loves animals almost as much as I do. She reads a lot of books about autism so she can learn how we can all help Evan. She takes Evan to his appointments and therapies and gets me to Brownie meetings and skating lessons.

My Mom gave me the idea to write this book because kids need to learn more about autism. I am the expert in my classroom on autism.

My Dad loves computers. He loves computers as much as Evan loves sticks. He also likes to hike and climb mountains. He likes to build things, too. He built a swing set for Evan and me to swing on. He loves to swing Evan really high into the sky. Evan loves it, too.

My brother and I love to play outdoors in the nice weather. Evan is hard to play with sometimes because he would rather flick a stick than play a game. I feel bad that he never has play dates. I could not live without playing with my friends. It is hard to understand what makes a stick so interesting. Maybe one day he will tell us.

I like to teach Evan things. He has a lot to learn from me and I am his best teacher. He learns more from me than from his teachers. I love Evan very much. I am his best friend.

Evan loves to swim. He always laughs and smiles in the pool. Swimming makes him happy. His therapist says Evan gets "sensory input" in the pool. All I know is that he has fun and we have fun together in the pool. We blow bubbles and splash each other. Evan is a really good swimmer.

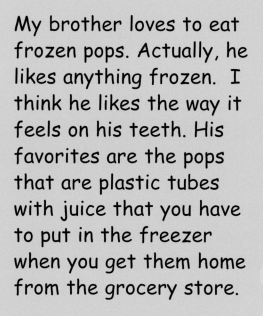

My brother loves to eat frozen pops. Actually, he likes anything frozen. I think he likes the way it feels on his teeth. His favorites are the pops that are plastic tubes with juice that you have to put in the freezer when you get them home from the grocery store.

Evan's speech thera-
pist, Ann, and I taught
Evan a game called
"the puffy cheeks
game." Evan puffs his
cheeks and fills them with
air and then we pop his cheeks and the air streams out. He likes other people to
do this to him and he pops other people's cheeks, too. Ann calls this an "oral
motor exercise." All I know is that Evan likes it and that it is fun for me, too.

Evan loves to take baths. I think he is part mermaid or something because he is happiest in water. One day he got in the tub and ran the water until the tub overflowed. There was water everywhere by the time my Mom realized what he had done. It was raining in the dining room and the water was coming down from the kitchen ceiling, too. It was a real mess, but Evan seemed to enjoy the whole thing. He often says funny sounds in the tub. His favorite is Ninga, Ninga. I haven't figured out what it means exactly, but it usually means that he is happy.

Evan loves to swing. I can swing with him or he can swing alone. Swinging makes him happy. He goes really high in the air. He never gets afraid. The higher, the better. Sometimes it looks like he is flying.

Home Trainer

Home Trainer

Evan has a home trainer coming to the house after school three afternoons a week. Her name is Jaimee, and she is really nice. Sometimes we all play together and I help her teach Evan. Not many kids know what a home trainer is. I had to explain it to my friends at school. One of them thought Evan had a personal trainer when I mentioned the term. In a way that's true. Evan's home trainer helps him learn all the things he needs to know.

What I want most for my brother is for him to learn to talk. Maybe he will some day, but even if he doesn't, I want him to know that I love him very much and that I will always be there for him, especially if he needs someone to laugh with.

Evan loves potato chips. He loves anything crunchy. His other favorite snack is raw pasta. He loves to crunch it on his teeth. The dentist said it is actually good for his teeth. The pasta works the same way as Daniel's biscuits in keeping Evan's teeth clean.

Sometimes Evan can be really annoying. I showed him how to feed my goldfish one day, and the next day he went into my room and opened the goldfish food and dumped the entire container into the tank. I was so mad! The goldfish was pretty upset, too. It was a real mess. Evan did not understand that goldfish only need a little food.

Most of the time, Evan doesn't like to wear clothes. I think it is because they feel uncomfortable against his skin. His favorite thing is to wear baggy boxer shorts. He also likes to wear my mother's gym shorts, which are also baggy and comfortable. When Evan comes home from school, he usually takes his clothes off and slips into his boxers to relax and kick back.

15

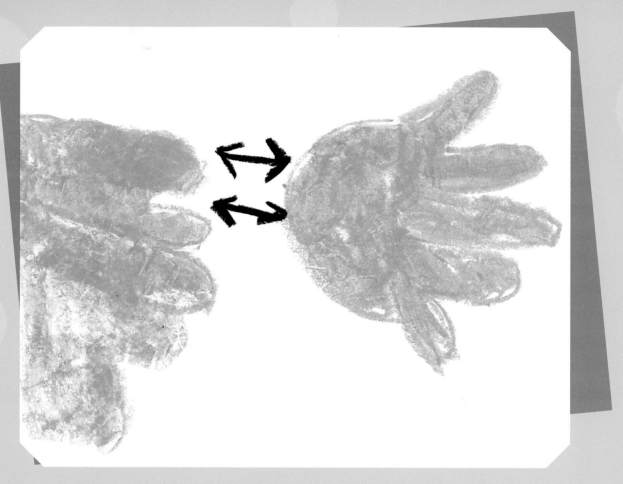

I love to teach my brother. He needs to learn so much about the world and I think that I do the best job teaching him. It is frustrating because you have to show him how to do things over and over again. Showing him once is not enough.

One day I taught my brother how to clap. Now whenever he sees me clap, he claps too. His teacher calls this "motor imitation." All I know is that Evan smiles when we clap together and that we have fun.

Evan also loves to jump on the bed and laugh. The therapists say he is getting "sensory input" by doing that, but what I know is that it is fun for both of us. He laughs so hard when he sees me jumping, too. Evan has a great laugh and we all love to hear it whenever we can.

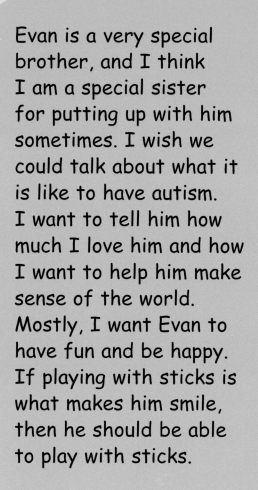

Evan is a very special brother, and I think I am a special sister for putting up with him sometimes. I wish we could talk about what it is like to have autism. I want to tell him how much I love him and how I want to help him make sense of the world. Mostly, I want Evan to have fun and be happy. If playing with sticks is what makes him smile, then he should be able to play with sticks.

LET'S STAY IN TOUCH

I would like to hear from you. If you have a brother or sister with autism, or if there is a student in your class with autism, let us share ideas for how we can help them.

My email address is: **sarah@asperger.net**

I can't wait to hear from you!

-Sarah

Draw and write your own stories

_____

_____

_____

_____

Draw and write your own stories

_____

_____

_____

_____

Draw and write your own stories

_____

_____

_____

_____